$30.00

HOCKEY SUPER STATS

JEFF SAVAGE

Lerner Publications ◆ Minneapolis

Stats are through the 2015–2016 NHL season.

Lerner Publications Company
A division of Lerner Publishing Group, Inc.
241 First Avenue North
Minneapolis, MN 55401 USA

For reading levels and more information, look up this title at www.lernerbooks.com.

Main body text set in Aptifer Sans LT Pro 12/18.
Typeface provided by Linotype AG.

Library of Congress Cataloging-in-Publication Data

Names: Savage, Jeff, 1961– author.
Title: Hockey Super Stats / Jeff Savage.
Description: Minneapolis, Minnesota : Lerner Publications, 2017. | Series: Pro Sports
    Stats | Includes bibliographical references and index. | Audience: Age 8–12. |
    Audience: Grade 4 to 6.
Identifiers: LCCN 2016046979 (print) | LCCN 2016054910 (ebook) | ISBN 9781512434118
    (lb : alk. paper) | ISBN 9781512449471 (eb pdf)
Subjects: LCSH: Hockey—Records—Juvenile literature. | Hockey—History—Juvenile
    literature.
Classification: LCC GV847.5 .S29 2017 (print) | LCC GV847.5 (ebook) | DDC 796.962—dc23

LC record available at https://lccn.loc.gov/2016046979

Manufactured in the United States of America
1-42047-23917-1/20/2017

TABLE OF CONTENTS

FROM THIN ICE TO SOLID

On December 19, 1917, exactly one minute into the first National Hockey League (NHL) game, defenseman Dave Ritchie scored a goal for the Montreal Wanderers. This was the first statistic, or stat, recorded in league history. Since then a wildly popular league has emerged. Its history is filled with fascinating and fun-to-read statistics. Fans use these stats to analyze and compare the performances of players and teams. Stats can help fans get information that may not be easy to see in a fast-paced game. To better understand hockey's important stats, it's helpful to know about the sport's history. Changes to rules, equipment, and rosters have all had an impact on hockey stats.

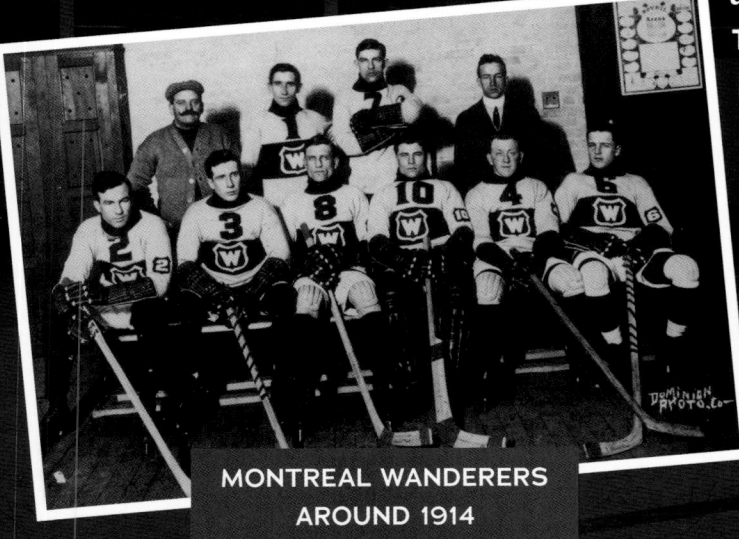

MONTREAL WANDERERS
AROUND 1914

OH, CANADA

Hockey's roots are in Canada. The first organized hockey game was played March 3, 1875, in Montreal, Quebec. There were nine players per side, and most were college students. Soon teams and leagues began to form, and in 1909, the National Hockey Association (NHA) was founded. It had seven teams in Ontario and Quebec. Eight years later, the NHA became the NHL.

Teams joined the league. Others folded. In 1942 the NHL had only six teams—the Boston Bruins, Chicago Blackhawks, Montreal Canadiens, New York Rangers, Toronto Maple Leafs, and Detroit Red Wings. These teams, later known as the Original Six, represented the league for the next 25 seasons. But when a Las Vegas team is added in 2017–2018, the league will consist of 31 teams. Not surprisingly, teams that have existed the longest have an advantage in all-time team statistics such as wins and Stanley Cup titles.

TORONTO MAPLE LEAFS VS. DETROIT RED WINGS IN 1942

CHAPTER ONE

PLAYER SUPER STATS

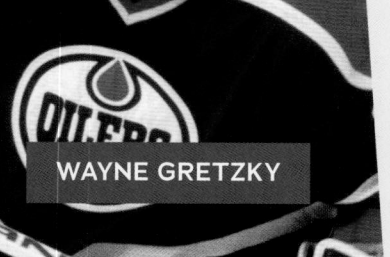

WAYNE GRETZKY

RACKING UP NUMBERS

In the 1944–1945 season, Maurice Richard scored 50 goals in 50 games for the Montreal Canadiens. For the next 30 years, it looked as if no one would be able to repeat—or beat—this scoring record. Finally, in 1980–1981, New York Islanders forward Mike Bossy achieved 50 in 50. Then, just one season later, Wayne Gretzky shattered the record, scoring 50 goals in just 39 games for the Edmonton Oilers. By the end of the season, Gretzky had scored 92 goals.

Most Goals Scored in a Career

PLAYER	TEAM*	GOALS
Wayne Gretzky	Edmonton Oilers	894
Gordie Howe	Detroit Red Wings	801
Jaromir Jagr	Pittsburgh Penguins	749
Brett Hull	St. Louis Blues	741
Marcel Dionne	Los Angeles Kings	731
Phil Esposito	Boston Bruins	717
Mike Gartner	Washington Capitals	708
Mark Messier	Edmonton Oilers	694
Steve Yzerman	Detroit Red Wings	692
Mario Lemieux	Pittsburgh Penguins	690

*The player spent most of his career with this team.

SCORING FRENZY

Joe Malone began playing for the Montreal Canadiens in 1917. Malone scored five goals in his first game. He scored again in his second game and then again in his third. In fact, Joe Malone, known as Phantom, scored at least one goal in each of his first 14 games! That's still the longest goal-scoring streak to begin a career in NHL history. Malone finished the season with 44 goals, an incredible 2.2 goals per game—a record that still stands. He was the league's first single-season scoring leader.

JOE MALONE

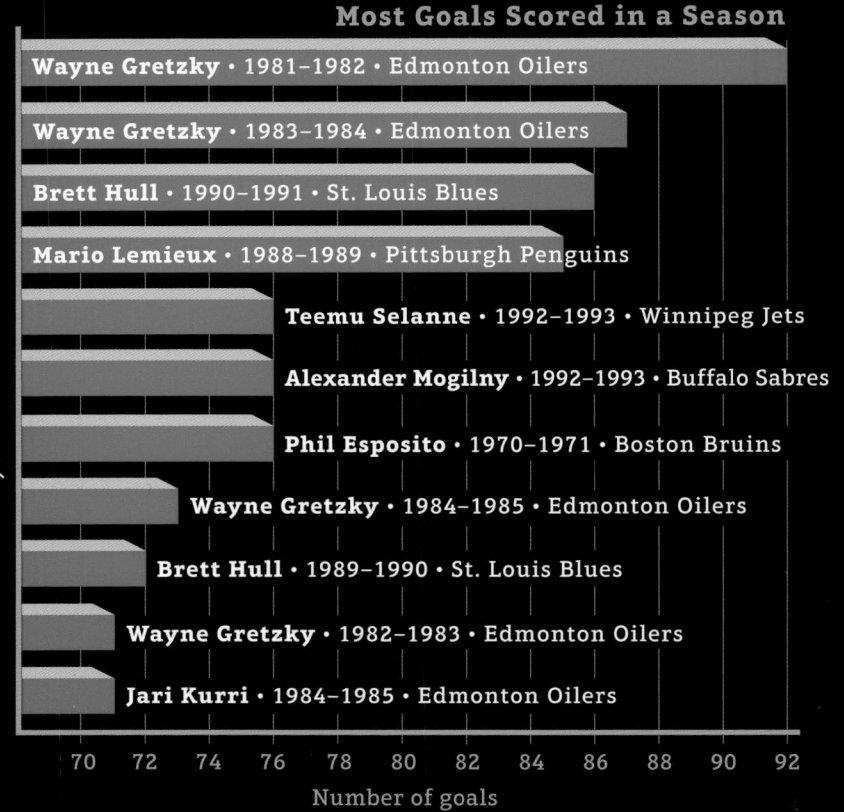

Most Goals Scored in a Season

Player • Season • Team*

Wayne Gretzky • 1981–1982 • Edmonton Oilers

Wayne Gretzky • 1983–1984 • Edmonton Oilers

Brett Hull • 1990–1991 • St. Louis Blues

Mario Lemieux • 1988–1989 • Pittsburgh Penguins

Teemu Selanne • 1992–1993 • Winnipeg Jets

Alexander Mogilny • 1992–1993 • Buffalo Sabres

Phil Esposito • 1970–1971 • Boston Bruins

Wayne Gretzky • 1984–1985 • Edmonton Oilers

Brett Hull • 1989–1990 • St. Louis Blues

Wayne Gretzky • 1982–1983 • Edmonton Oilers

Jari Kurri • 1984–1985 • Edmonton Oilers

70 72 74 76 78 80 82 84 86 88 90 92

Number of goals

JAROMIR JAGR

GAME-WINNING GOALS

Some goals are more important than others. For example, the goal that gives a team the lead after the game has been tied is called the go-ahead goal. It's more important than, say, a goal scored with a 5–1 lead. Scoring a goal to break a tie game is a big deal. But it's even more exciting when the game-winning goal is scored in **overtime**!

Most Career Game-Winning Goals

PLAYER	TEAM*	GOALS
Jaromir Jagr	Pittsburgh Penguins	133
Phil Esposito	Boston Bruins	118
Brett Hull	St. Louis Blues	110
Teemu Selanne	Anaheim Ducks	110
Brendan Shanahan	Detroit Red Wings	109
Jarome Iginla	Calgary Flames	97
Guy Lafleur	Montreal Canadiens	97
Mats Sundin	Toronto Maple Leafs	96
Steve Yzerman	Detroit Red Wings	94

*The player spent most of his career with this team.

DO YOU LIKE MY HAT?

During a March 24, 2016, game between the Minnesota Wild and the Calgary Flames, Minnesota's Zach Parise redirected a shot to score a goal. It was Parise's third goal of the game—he had scored a **hat trick**!

Hat tricks are most commonly recorded in hockey and soccer. According to the Hockey Hall of Fame, the first hockey hat trick was in 1946 when player Alex Kaleta could not afford to buy a hat in a store. The store owner said Kaleta could have the hat if he scored three goals in a game that night. Kaleta scored four goals and got the hat. In the 2015–2016 season, 67 hat tricks were recorded.

STATS FACT

Joe Malone is the only player to ever score seven goals in a game. He did it for the Quebec Bulldogs in their final game of the 1919–1920 season.

Hat Trick Leaders in 2015–2016

Zach Parise · Minnesota Wild

Mikkel Boedker · Colorado Avalanche

Filip Forsberg · Nashville Predators

Michael Frolik · Calgary Flames

Johnny Gaudreau · Calgary Flames

Patrick Kane · Chicago Blackhawks

Alex Ovechkin · Washington Capitals

Jeff Skinner · Carolina Hurricanes

Jason Spezza · Dallas Stars

Player · Team

0   1   2   3

Number of hat tricks

MARIO LEMIEUX

A LITTLE HELP, PLEASE

Hockey rewards teamwork. In basketball and soccer, the player who passes the ball to a scoring teammate is credited with an assist. But in hockey, assists are often given to two players. The last two offensive players to shoot, **deflect**, or otherwise touch the puck before a goal are given assists. Wayne Gretzky and Mario Lemieux are widely considered two of the greatest passers ever—and they have great assist stats to back it up.

STATS FACT

On February 6, 1976, Darryl Sittler of the Toronto Maple Leafs scored 10 points in a game, with five goals and five assists. The next highest single-game point total in history is eight.

Most Assists per Games Played in a Career

PLAYER	TEAM*	ASSISTS PER GAMES PLAYED
Wayne Gretzky	Edmonton Oilers	1.32
Mario Lemieux	Pittsburgh Penguins	1.13
Bobby Orr	Boston Bruins	0.98
Peter Forsberg	Colorado Avalanche	0.90
Sidney Crosby	Pittsburgh Penguins	0.85
Peter Stastny	Quebec Nordiques	0.81
Adam Oates	Boston Bruins	0.81
Paul Coffey	Edmonton Oilers	0.81
Marcel Dionne	Los Angeles Kings	0.77
Kent Nilsson	Calgary Flames	0.76

*The player spent most of his career with this team.

POINTS

In hockey an assist is considered to be just as valuable as a goal. One point is added to a player's individual stats for a goal or for an assist. At the end of each season, the leader in points receives the Art Ross Trophy, which was named for the former player, coach, and general manager who also designed the NHL puck. It's easier to get an assist than a goal—the Art Ross Trophy has only been awarded to a player with more goals than assists nine times.

Art Ross Trophy Winners

Player • Team*

Wayne Gretzky • Edmonton Oilers
Gordie Howe • Detroit Red Wings
Mario Lemieux • Pittsburgh Penguins
Phil Esposito • Boston Bruins
Jaromir Jagr • Pittsburgh Penguins
Stan Mikita • Chicago Blackhawks
Bobby Hull • Chicago Blackhawks
Guy Lafleur • Montreal Canadiens
Sidney Crosby • Pittsburgh Penguins
Bernie Geoffrion • Montreal Canadiens
Evgeni Malkin • Pittsburgh Penguins
Dickie Moore • Montreal Canadiens
Bobby Orr • Boston Bruins
Martin St. Louis • Tampa Bay Lightning

0 1 2 3 4 5 6 7 8 9 10
Number of Art Ross Trophies

*The player spent most of his career with this team.

PHIL ESPOSITO

STATS FACT
In 1968–1969, Phil Esposito of the Boston Bruins became the first player to record more than 100 points in a season. In 74 games, he had 49 goals and 77 assists for 126 points.

MAKING THEIR POINT

It takes great skill to be ranked among hockey's all-time points leaders. Of the 30 players with the most points of all time, 25 are in hockey's Hall of Fame. Being near the top of the all-time points list also takes a long playing career. Gordie Howe, nicknamed Mr. Hockey, played in the NHL for 26 seasons and was a 52-year-old grandfather when he finally retired. The top 10 players on the NHL's all-time points list each played for at least 18 seasons.

GORDIE HOWE

All-Time Points Leaders

PLAYER	TEAM*	CAREER	POINTS
Wayne Gretzky	Edmonton Oilers	1979–1999	2,857
Mark Messier	Edmonton Oilers	1979–2004	1,887
Jaromir Jagr	Pittsburgh Penguins	1990–2017	1,868
Gordie Howe	Detroit Red Wings	1946–1980	1,850
Ron Francis	Hartford Whalers	1981–2004	1,798
Marcel Dionne	Los Angeles Kings	1971–1989	1,771
Steve Yzerman	Detroit Red Wings	1983–2006	1,755
Mario Lemieux	Pittsburgh Penguins	1984–2006	1,723
Joe Sakic	Colorado Avalanche	1988–2009	1,641
Phil Esposito	Boston Bruins	1963–1981	1,590

*The player spent most of his career with this team.

THE PUCK STOPS HERE

A hockey goal is 4 feet (1.2 meters) high and 6 feet (1.8 m) wide. The goalie's job is to protect that space in any way possible. Standing in front of a 100-mile-per-hour (160-kilometer) **slap shot** takes courage. Actually stopping the puck takes quickness and agility. In hockey's early years, goalies were not allowed to drop to the ice, and they wore very little equipment. They didn't even wear helmets or masks! In recent years, the NHL has featured bigger, better equipment and more skilled goaltenders, resulting in lower-scoring games. Of the 10 goalies with the most wins in NHL history, seven led their teams to at least one Stanley Cup title.

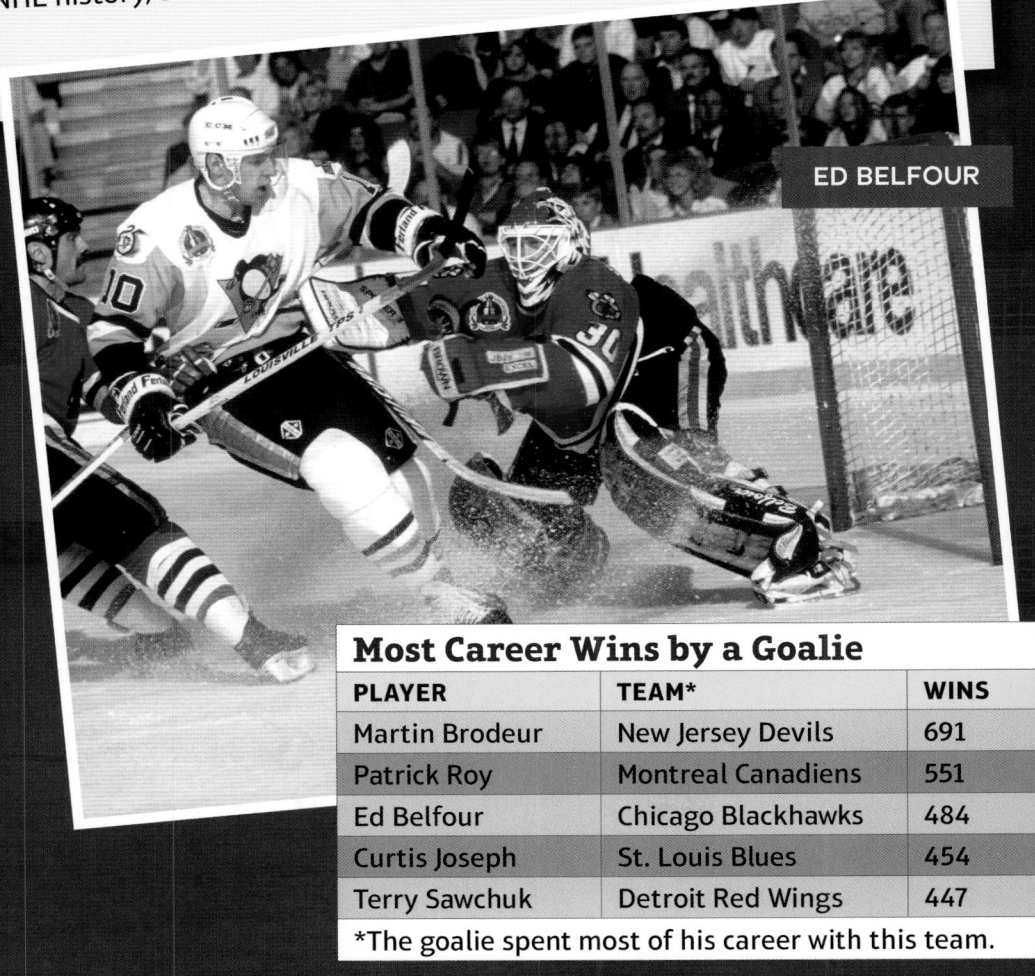

ED BELFOUR

Most Career Wins by a Goalie

PLAYER	TEAM*	WINS
Martin Brodeur	New Jersey Devils	691
Patrick Roy	Montreal Canadiens	551
Ed Belfour	Chicago Blackhawks	484
Curtis Joseph	St. Louis Blues	454
Terry Sawchuk	Detroit Red Wings	447

*The goalie spent most of his career with this team.

YOU GET NOTHING

A team might have good goal scorers, but without a great goalie to back them up, the team won't win a lot. One sure way to stay close in every game is to prevent the other team from scoring. In a playoff game on March 24, 1936, the Montreal Maroons fired shot after shot at Detroit Red Wings goalie Normie Smith. He stopped them all. The game went to six overtime periods. Smith faced 92 shots in the game. He made 92 **saves**, holding onto the **shutout** for nine periods. The Red Wings finally scored to win the longest game in NHL history.

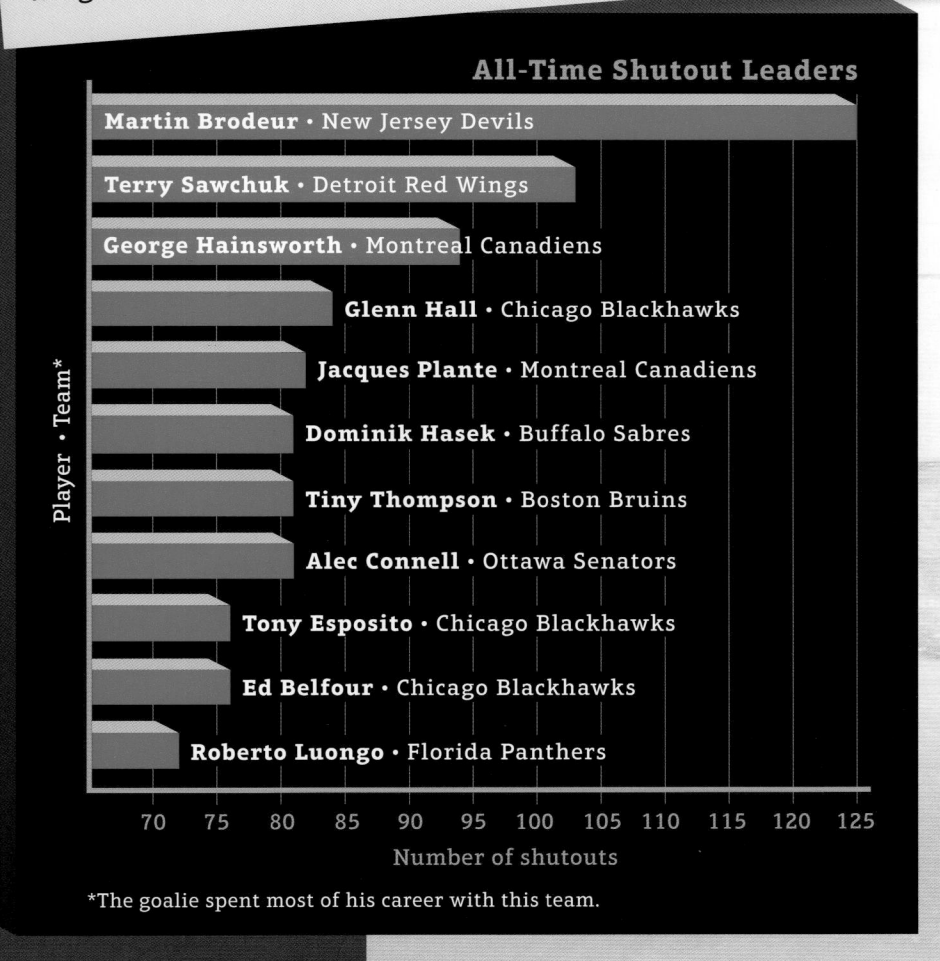

All-Time Shutout Leaders

Player • Team*

Martin Brodeur • New Jersey Devils
Terry Sawchuk • Detroit Red Wings
George Hainsworth • Montreal Canadiens
Glenn Hall • Chicago Blackhawks
Jacques Plante • Montreal Canadiens
Dominik Hasek • Buffalo Sabres
Tiny Thompson • Boston Bruins
Alec Connell • Ottawa Senators
Tony Esposito • Chicago Blackhawks
Ed Belfour • Chicago Blackhawks
Roberto Luongo • Florida Panthers

70 75 80 85 90 95 100 105 110 115 120 125
Number of shutouts

*The goalie spent most of his career with this team.

BRIAN BOUCHER

STATS FACT

Goaltender Brian Boucher
of the Phoenix Coyotes
recorded five consecutive
shutouts in the 2003–2004
season. It broke a record
that had stood for 55 years.

SERVING TIME

Referees give players penalties for breaking the rules. The offending player is sent to the penalty box for at least two minutes, and his team cannot send in a replacement. This leaves the team one player short. The other side has an advantage known as a power play. A minor penalty such as slashing an opponent with the stick is a two-minute penalty. A major penalty such as fighting is five minutes. Misconduct penalties are 10 minutes. The player is sent off the ice, but the team can send in a replacement during this time.

Penalties can affect the outcome of a game by giving a team more opportunities to score, but penalties also change the mood in an arena. Fights add excitement for fans and often give teams a boost in energy—even if their players end up in the penalty box.

TIGER WILLIAMS
(RIGHT)

STATS FACT

The first player to get more than 300 penalty minutes in a season was Philadelphia Flyers forward Dave Schultz with 348 in 1973–1974. The next year, he got 472, which is still the most ever.

Most Career Penalty Minutes

PLAYER	TEAM*	MINUTES
Tiger Williams	Toronto Maple Leafs	3,966
Dale Hunter	Washington Capitals	3,565
Tie Domi	Toronto Maple Leafs	3,515
Marty McSorley	Los Angeles Kings	3,381
Bob Probert	Detroit Red Wings	3,300
Rob Ray	Buffalo Sabres	3,207
Craig Berube	Washington Capitals	3,149
Tim Hunter	Calgary Flames	3,146
Chris Nilan	Montreal Canadiens	3,043
Rick Tocchet	Philadelphia Flyers	2,972

*The player spent most of his career with this team.

THE MOST VALUABLE MVP

At the end of each regular season, a large group of reporters known as the Professional Hockey Writers Association votes for the player who is most valuable to his team. The winner receives the Hart Memorial Trophy. Wayne Gretzky won the Most Valuable Player (MVP) award nine times. This is more MVP awards than any other player in any major sport has received.

HISTORY HIGHLIGHT

No athlete dominated a sport more than Wayne Gretzky dominated hockey. Gretzky, or the Great One, holds 61 NHL records, the most by far. Gretzky has more *assists* than any other player has goals and assists *combined*. Perhaps his greatest stat of all? Gretzky's jersey number (99) was retired by every team in the NHL!

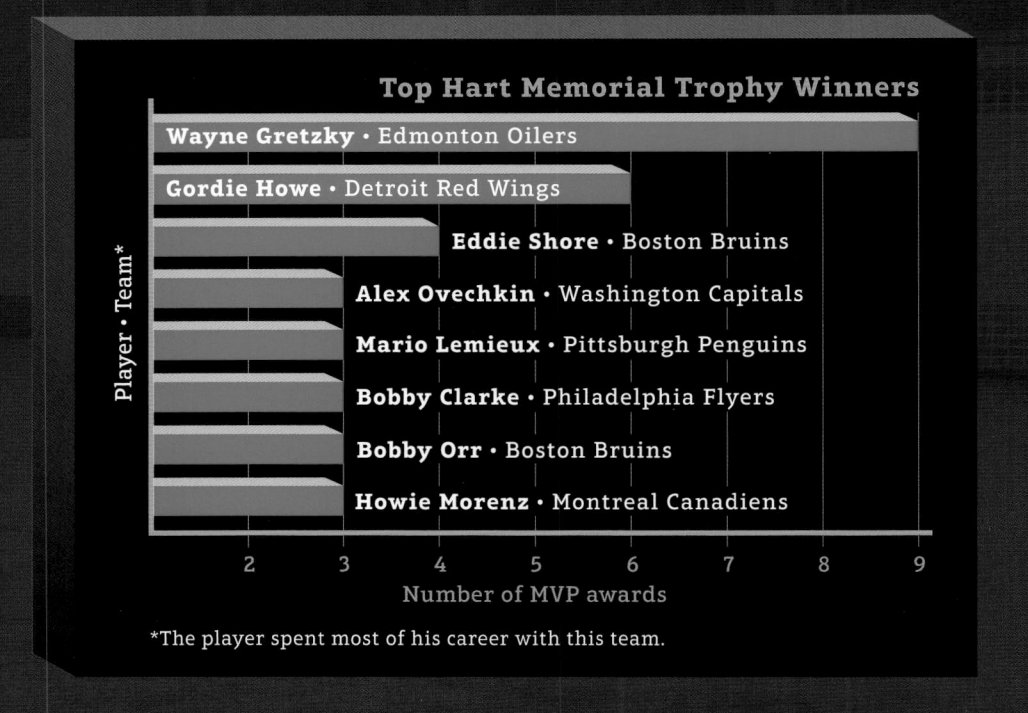

Top Hart Memorial Trophy Winners

Wayne Gretzky • Edmonton Oilers
Gordie Howe • Detroit Red Wings
Eddie Shore • Boston Bruins
Alex Ovechkin • Washington Capitals
Mario Lemieux • Pittsburgh Penguins
Bobby Clarke • Philadelphia Flyers
Bobby Orr • Boston Bruins
Howie Morenz • Montreal Canadiens

Player • Team*

2 3 4 5 6 7 8 9
Number of MVP awards

*The player spent most of his career with this team.

CHAPTER TWO

TEAM SUPER STATS

IT'S ALL ABOUT WINNING

The Presidents' Trophy (*right*) is awarded to the NHL team that finishes the regular season with the best record. That team is guaranteed **home ice advantage** as long as they last in the playoffs. But having the best regular season record doesn't guarantee playoff success. In the 30 years since the Presidents' Trophy was introduced in 1985–1986, only eight teams have won the trophy and the Stanley Cup in the same season.

Best Regular Season Records since 1985–1986

SEASON	TEAM	POINTS	PLAYOFF RESULT
1995–1996	Detroit Red Wings	131	Lost in Conference Final
2005–2006	Detroit Red Wings	124	Lost in First Round
2009–2010	Washington Capitals	121	Lost in First Round
2015–2016	Washington Capitals	120	Lost in Second Round
1992–1993	Pittsburgh Penguins	119	Lost in Second Round
1985–1986	Edmonton Oilers	119	Lost in Second Round
2000–2001	Colorado Avalanche	118	Won Stanley Cup
2013–2014	Boston Bruins	117	Lost in Second Round
2010–2011	Vancouver Canucks	117	Lost Stanley Cup
2008–2009	San Jose Sharks	117	Lost in First Round
1988–1989	Calgary Flames	117	Won Stanley Cup

EXPAND YOUR HORIZONS

The Minnesota Wild and Columbus Blue Jackets were newly formed teams in 2000. In the next 16 years, the Wild made the playoffs seven times—not bad for an **expansion team**. The Jackets reached the postseason only two times. The Detroit Red Wings, however, made the playoffs for the 25th year straight in 2015–2016. The last time the Red Wings missed the playoffs, almost half of their current players had not even been born!

2016 MINNESOTA WILD

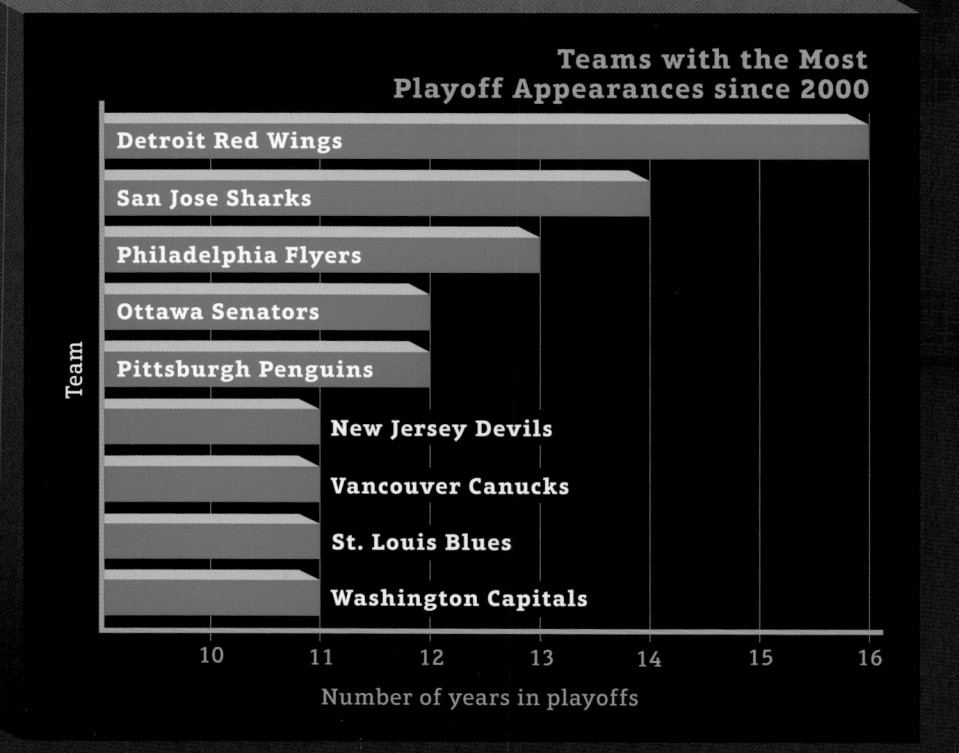

Teams with the Most Playoff Appearances since 2000

Team	Number of years in playoffs
Detroit Red Wings	16
San Jose Sharks	14
Philadelphia Flyers	13
Ottawa Senators	12
Pittsburgh Penguins	12
New Jersey Devils	11
Vancouver Canucks	11
St. Louis Blues	11
Washington Capitals	11

HOISTING THE CUP!

The goal of every NHL player is to hoist the Stanley Cup and skate with it around the ice after winning the championship. The trophy is named after former Canadian governor general Frederick Arthur Stanley. Stanley awarded the cup to Canada's top-ranked amateur hockey team, the Montreal Amateur Athletic Association, in 1893. The original cup was 7 inches (18 centimeters) high. In 1926–1927, the cup became the prize for the top NHL team. Each year the names of the players, coaches, and staff of the winning team are etched on a ring at the base of the cup. After the 2015–2016 season, the cup was more than 35 inches (89 cm) tall and weighed nearly 35 pounds (16 kilograms).

MATT CULLEN
WITH THE STANLEY CUP IN 2016

HISTORY HIGHLIGHT

Mario Lemieux was a great scorer who refused to quit. He led the Pittsburgh Penguins to back-to-back Stanley Cups in 1990–1991 and 1991–1992. In 1992–1993, Lemieux was on his way to setting an NHL scoring record when he was diagnosed with cancer. He still won the Art Ross Trophy that season, but he missed most of the 1993–1994 season and all of 1994–1995. By the time he retired in 1997, he had won the Art Ross Trophy six times. But he still wasn't done with the game. In 2000 Lemieux came out of retirement and played until 2006.

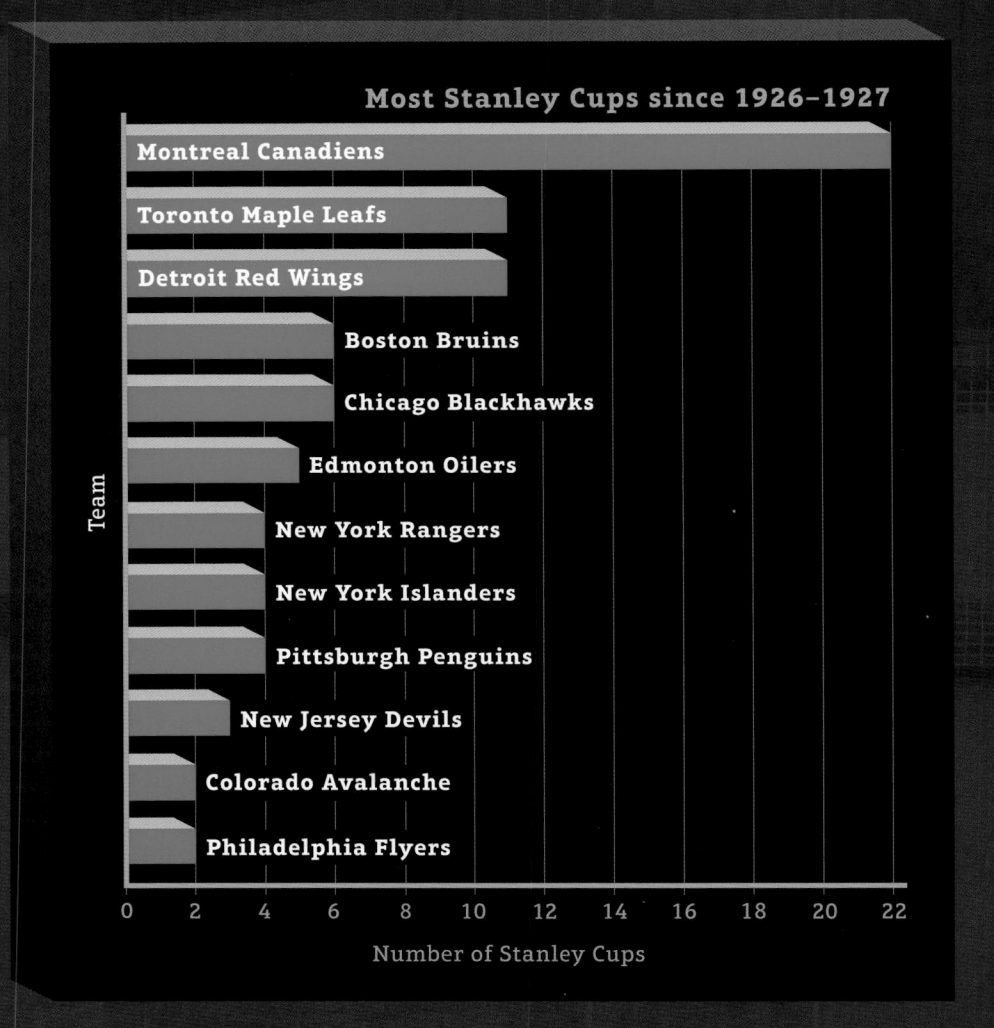

Most Stanley Cups since 1926–1927

STREAK!

Winning is a habit. But so is losing. A team on a winning streak will be filled with confidence, which leads to more winning. On the other hand, a team that can't seem to win a game is seized by pressure, which often leads to more losing. That's the mental side of hockey. On the physical side, some teams simply have better players than others.

1975–1976 The Kansas City Scouts record was 12 wins, 56 losses, and 12 ties (12–56–12). At one point, they went 27 straight games without winning.

1975–1976 In their first season (1974–1975), the Washington Capitals finished with an 8–67–5 record, the worst NHL record of all time. Their second season wasn't much better. They won 11 games. But they also went 25 games in a row without a win.

1977–1978 The Montreal Canadiens went on a 28-game undefeated streak on their way to hoisting the cup. They dominated the decade, winning the Stanley Cup six times in the 1970s.

1979–1980 The Philadelphia Flyers were a team of tough players known as the Broad Street Bullies. The Flyers played so rough that seven players each racked up 100-plus minutes of penalties for the season. Despite so much time in the penalty box, the Flyers went on a record-breaking 35-game winning streak.

1980–1981 The Winnipeg Jets won 20 games during their first season in the NHL (1979–1980). Then, in their second year, the Jets finished 9–57–14. Their miserable season included a 30-game losing streak.

1992–1993 The Pittsburgh Penguins seemed to be on their way to a third straight Stanley Cup title as they achieved 17 straight victories and captured the Presidents' Trophy. But they lost in the second round of the playoffs.

LIGHTING THE LAMP

When a goal is scored, a red light behind the net flashes on. Fans call this lighting the lamp. In the last decade, only the Washington Capitals and the Buffalo Sabres have lit the lamp more than 300 times in a season. But throughout the 1970s and 1980s, it was common for teams to score more than 300 goals. In fact, teams have scored more than 300 goals 184 times in NHL history. That's a lot of lamp lighting!

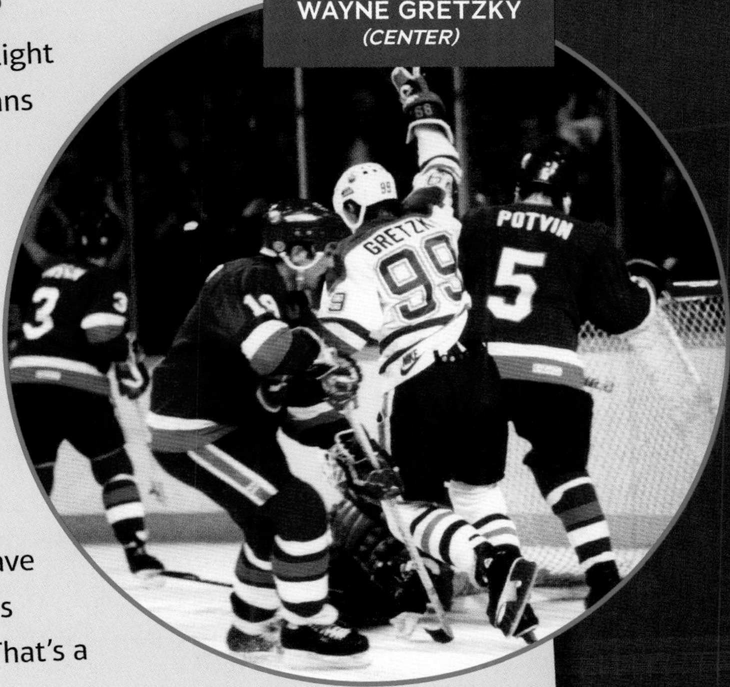

WAYNE GRETZKY
(CENTER)

Most Goals Scored in a Season		
SEASON	TEAM	GOALS SCORED
1983–1984	Edmonton Oilers	446
1985–1986	Edmonton Oilers	426
1982–1983	Edmonton Oilers	424
1981–1982	Edmonton Oilers	417
1984–1985	Edmonton Oilers	401
1970–1971	Boston Bruins	399
1987–1988	Calgary Flames	397
1976–1977	Montreal Canadiens	387
1981–1982	New York Islanders	385
1988–1989	Los Angeles Kings	376

CHAPTER THREE

STATS ARE HERE TO STAY

GAME SUMMARIES

One way to study and compare player and team stats is by looking at game summaries. In many sports, this summary is known as a box score, and it shows stats for each player in the game. Many sports also use a line score—a summary of the final score of the game.

In hockey, along with the line score and player stats, there is a summary of scoring and penalties, which shows who scored and who received penalties during each period of the game. Use the key to understand the final scoring summary and scoring/penalty summary on the next page.

Key

1 = first period

2 = second period

3 = third period

T = total goals

EV) = teams were at even strength, or had an equal number of players on the ice, at the time of the goal

PP) = the scoring team had a power play, or at least one extra skater on the ice, at the time of the goal

2:46 (example) = the time that had passed in the period

2) (example) = number of penalty minutes to be served

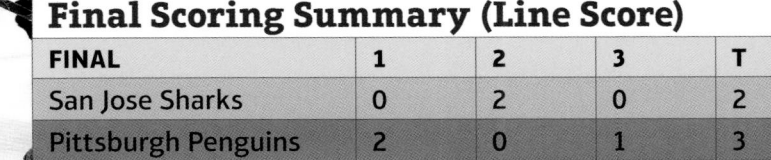

SAN JOSE SHARKS
VS.
PITTSBURGH PENGUINS

Final Scoring Summary (Line Score)

FINAL	1	2	3	T
San Jose Sharks	0	2	0	2
Pittsburgh Penguins	2	0	1	3

Scoring/Penalty Summary

First Period

SCORING

12:46 – Penguins Bryan Rust (EV) Assists: Justin Schultz, Chris Kunitz

13:48 – Penguins Conor Sheary (EV) Assists: Sidney Crosby, Olli Maatta

PENALTIES

8:54 – Sharks Dainius Zubrus (2) *High-sticking*

Second Period

SCORING

3:02 – Sharks Tomas Hertl (PP) Assists: Joonas Donskoi, Brent Burns

18:12 – Sharks Patrick Marleau (EV) Assists: Brent Burns, Logan Couture

PENALTIES

1:14 – Penguins Ian Cole (2) *Hooking*

18:52 – Penguins Evgeni Malkin (2) *Slashing*

18:52 – Sharks Joe Pavelski (2) *Tripping*

18:52 – Sharks Joe Thornton (2) *Roughing*

Third Period

SCORING

17:27 – Penguins Nick Bonino (EV) Assists: Kris Letang, Carl Hagelin

PENALTIES

4:47 – Sharks Patrick Marleau (2) *Illegal check to the head*

17:51 – Penguins Ben Lovejoy (2) *Hooking*

GAME ACTION

Fans love to study stats to compare players and teams. Players, coaches, and **agents** use stats too. Stats help teams decide which new players to draft and how much money to pay players. Stats also help players and coaches plan strategies for a game. For example, a shooter may aim a shot low between the pads of a goaltender or high to the stick side, depending on a goalie's **save percentage** in different areas of the net. The goalie might adjust his position and angle based on who has the puck and whether the player is statistically likely to pass or shoot.

Coaches also use statistics to decide who will play certain games. For example, goaltenders that play two nights in a row usually have a lower save percentage the second night, so the coach may decide to go with the backup goalie instead.

FANTASY AND THE FUTURE

Some adult fans want to get even more involved with the stats of their favorite players and teams. In fantasy hockey leagues, fans draft players to form teams. Fantasy teams earn points based on the real statistics of NHL players. Fans can add, drop, or trade players to improve their teams. One study showed that 56.8 million people in the United States and Canada played fantasy sports in 2015.

As the popularity of stats has grown, NHL teams have started to hire analysts to study statistics. These analysts help players and teams come up with new strategies. Microchips are being placed in jerseys and pucks to track players and provide even more statistics to study. Teams can track the precise location on the ice of each player and the puck, as well as the speed at which they move. These statistics will help players and fans understand how puck handling, power play minutes, and more all work together to make up a great game.

STATS MATCHUP

Alex Ovechkin and Sidney Crosby both entered the NHL in 2005–2006. Ovechkin is a shooter. He led the league in shots taken during 10 of his first 11 seasons! He led the league in goals scored six times.

ALEX OVECHKIN

Alex Ovechkin Washington Capitals	
839	Games played
4,228	Shots
525	Goals
.626	Goals per game
441	Assists
.526	Assists per game
966	Points
1.151	Points per game
88	Game-winning goals
3	MVPs
0	Stanley Cup titles

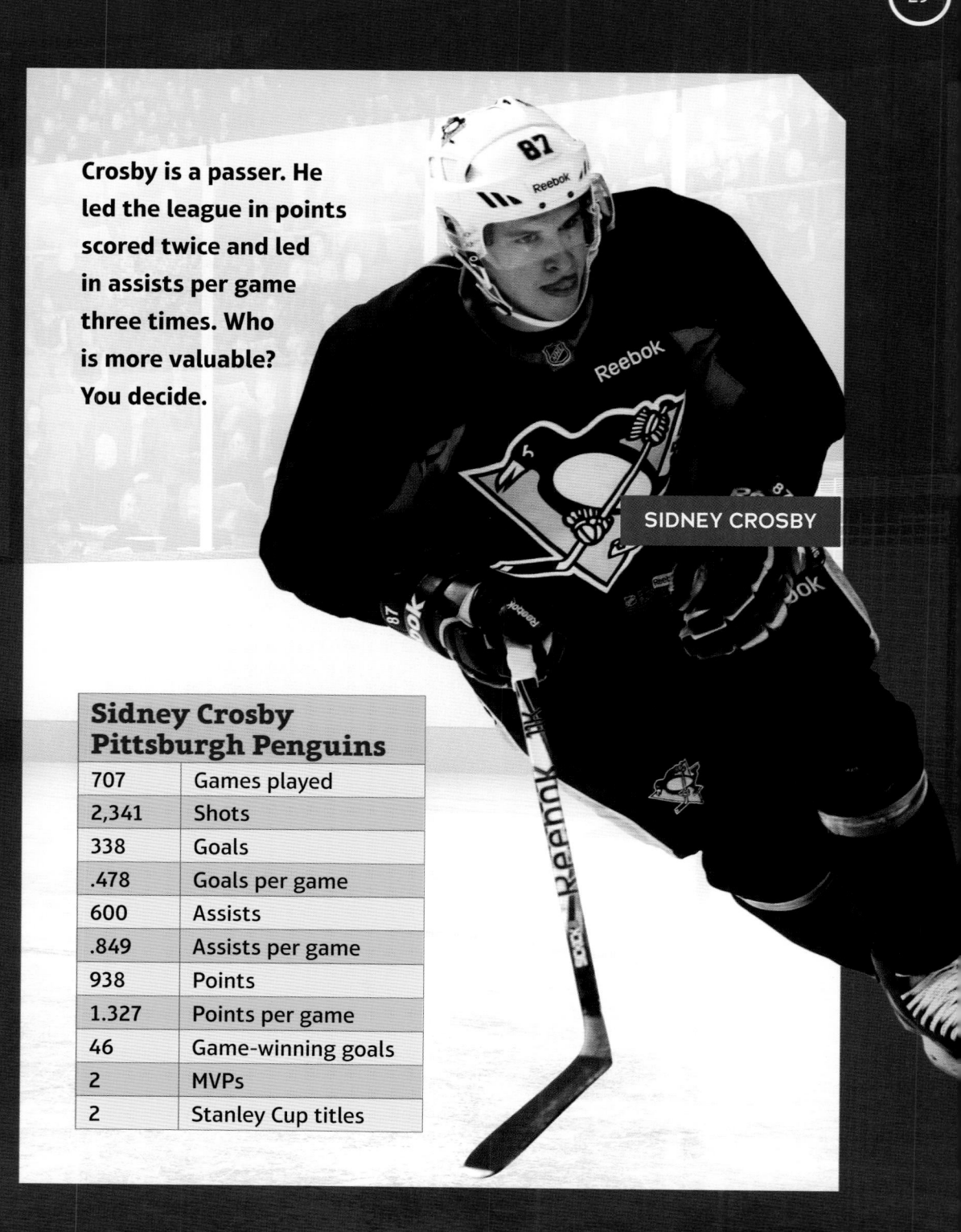

Crosby is a passer. He led the league in points scored twice and led in assists per game three times. Who is more valuable? You decide.

SIDNEY CROSBY

Sidney Crosby Pittsburgh Penguins	
707	Games played
2,341	Shots
338	Goals
.478	Goals per game
600	Assists
.849	Assists per game
938	Points
1.327	Points per game
46	Game-winning goals
2	MVPs
2	Stanley Cup titles

GLOSSARY

agents: people who represent players, mainly for matters involving money, such as negotiating a contract with a team

deflect: to redirect a shot

expansion team: a newly formed team in a sports league, usually in a city that has not had a team in that league before

hat trick: three goals scored by one player in a game

home ice advantage: playing more games at home than on the road during the playoffs

overtime: a five-minute extra period that is played when the third period ends in a tie. The period ends if either team scores.

save percentage: a statistic that measures a goalkeeper's ability. It is calculated by dividing total goals by shots on goal.

saves: a statistic for a goalkeeper who prevents shots on goal from crossing the goal line

shutout: a game in which one team does not score any goals

slap shot: the fastest shot in hockey, made when a player takes a full backswing to wind up for a shot

FURTHER INFORMATION

ESPN Hockey
http://www.espn.com/nhl/statistics

Herman, Gail. *Who Is Wayne Gretzky?* New York: Grosset & Dunlap, 2015.

Hockey Reference
http://www.hockey-reference.com

National Hockey League
https://www.nhl.com

Savage, Jeff. *Super Hockey Infographics.* Minneapolis: Lerner Publications, 2015.

Tejada, Justin. *Sports Illustrated Kids Stats! The Greatest Numbers in Sports.* New York: Time Home Entertainment, 2013.

INDEX

PHOTO ACKNOWLEDGMENTS

The images in this book are used with the permission of: © iStockphoto.com/Dmytro Aksonov (hockey rink background throughout); © iStockphoto.com/peepo, p. 1; © B Bennett/Bruce Bennett/Getty Images, pp. 4, 6, 7 (Joe Malone), 12, 15; © Conn Smythe Fonds/Wikimedia Commons (public domain), p. 5; © Laura Westlund/ Independent Picture Service, pp. 7, 9, 11, 14, 17, 19, 21 (graph); © Denis Brodeur/ National Hockey League/Getty Images, p. 8; AP Photo/Gene J. Puskar, p. 10; © B Bennett/Contributor/Getty Images Sport Classic/Getty Images, p. 11; © Bruce Bennett/Getty Images, p. 13; © Steve Babineau/National Hockey League/Getty Images, p. 16; © Dave Reginek/National Hockey League/Getty Images, p. 18; © Bruce Kluckhohn/National Hockey League/Getty Images, p. 19 (Minnesota Wild); © Dave Sandford/National Hockey League/Getty Images, pp. 20, 25; © Focus On Sport/Getty Images, p. 23; © dotshock/Shutterstock.com, p. 26; © Jacob Lund/Shutterstock. com, p. 27; © Josh Chapel/Southcreek/ZUMA Press, Inc./Alamy, p. 28; © CHRISTINNE MUSCHI/REUTERS/Alamy, p. 29.

Front cover: © iStockphoto.com/peepo.